ON THE LEVEL

also by Bryan R. Monte

Tiny Zion

ON THE LEVEL

Bryan R. Monte

BRYAN R. MONTE
POEMS ON LIVING
WITH MULTIPLE SCLEROSIS

CIRCLING RIVERS
RICHMOND, VIRGINIA

CIRCLING RIVERS

PO Box 8291
Richmond, VA 23226 USA

Visit CirclingRivers.com to subscribe to news of our authors and books, including book giveaways. We never share or sell our list.

ISBN: 978-1-939530-27-1 (paper)

ISBN: 978-1-939530-28-8 (hardcover)

Library of Congress Control Number: 2022935106

Cover art: *Gelb-Rot-Blau* (Yellow-Red-Blue), by Vassily Kandinsky. Collection of Musée national d'art moderne, Centre Georges Pompidou, Paris. Photo of artwork: Centre Pompidou, MNAM-CCI/Adam Rzepka/Dist. RMN-GP.

Author photo copyright © María Minaya

This book is a creative work. It is not a medical guide. Please check with your physician and/or specialist concerning the exercises, medications, diagnostic tools, procedures, and treatments described herein.

For the Amsterdam Quarterly Writers' Group
and my Three Graces
Nonnie Augustine, Dianne Kellogg, and Meryl Stratford

Non nobis solum nati sumus
— Cicero, *De Officiis*

CONTENTS

Dedication | 5

Epigraph | 7

The ABCs of Multiple Sclerosis | 13

FIRST SIGNS

First Signs | 19

The Familiar Stranger | 20

These Legs | 21

After the Fall | 22

Just Two Steps | 23

…And That Very Same Evening | 25

Today I Forgot | 26

Here's Something for the Pain | 28

The Law of the Conservation of Anxiety | 30

BETHESDA

Bethesda | 35

Dress Oxfords | 37

The Braces | 38

Schwarzwälder Kirschtorte | 39

Winking through the Menthol | 41

Glasgow Meeting | 42

The Fire from Above | 44

The Rattle | 45

Burgundy | 47

Praatgroep | 48

Why I Like the Ballet | 50

Why I Hate Generics | 52

Morning Exercises | 53

Fall Training | 54

This House of Disabled People | 55

PATIENT SAYS "NO"

Patient Says "No" | 59

Don't Ask | 61

Side Effects | 62

Why I Have Fired My Therapists | 63

What TV Taught Me about MS | 64

Yet Another Cure | 65
The Object of their Lesson | 66

ON THE LEVEL

On the Level | 70
No One Ever Asks | 71
Nobody | 72
There Is a Difference | 73
Gravity | 75
Inertia | 76
The Rotor | 78
The Mask | 79
The Hug | 80
The Plug | 81
The Hotel Reading | 82
While We're All Still Here | 84
Suspended | 85
Why I Didn't Use the Back Door | 86
Your Wheelchair Is Too Wide | 89
Yellow-Red-Blue | 91
A Drive with Mondrian | 92

HOMECOMING

Homecoming | 97
First Cousins Once Removed | 99
Moonfaced Man | 100
Somewhere under Their Radar | 101
Trento | 103
For Whom We Are Born | 104
I'm So Tired of Floating | 107
The Escape Artist | 108
Thin Strips of Latex and Fabric | 109
À l'Apollinaire? | 110
The Way You Left | 112
One Room | 116
White Room | 117

Acknowledgments | 118

ON THE LEVEL

THE ABCS OF MULTIPLE SCLEROSIS

A is for *Aphasia, Apraxia,* and *Ataxia*
when I talk and walk
like a drunken man with a stroke.

B is for *Bowel* and *Bladder*
that, at the wrong time,
always seem to matter.

C is for *Catheter, Constipation,* and *Colon*
for things I *Can't* get out
or *Can't* keep in.

D is for *Demyelination* of nerve endings
Depression, Diplopia, Dizziness,
Dysphagia when pills won't go down,
or *Dysphonia* when I speak too loudly or off pitch.

E is for fewer *Ejaculations* and lots of *Energy* conservation
for *Exacerbations* and treatment *Experimentations,*
the last two of which I can do without.

F is for *Fatigue, Flaccidity,* and lack of *Fluency,*
and *Four, Forty-five-minute* work periods each day,
for *Foot braces* to correct my *Foot drop*
as I walk as I talk, with a limp, a hesitation.

G and H are for *Genetics* and *Grandma* Monte
from *wHom* I *inHerited* this partially *Hereditary* disease.
H is also for *Hydrotherapy* that strangely *Helps,*
and for *Hospitals* from *Hell* whose coffee and cakes
Heal better sometimes than their doctors.

I is for *Immune system, Impotence,*
and all the *"Ins"* I would rather be without—
Incontinence, Incoordination, Interferon
for *Internuclear ophthalmoplegia* and *cardiology*
to monitor the spasms of my eyes and heart.

J is for *Junior*, my *Jerky* young doctor,
a neurologist in training,
always *Jingling* his supervisor for advice,
my medical record his *Juvenilia.*

K is for *Klenzak braces*
that *Keep* me upright when I go into the city
with just my walker and cane.

L is for *Lots* of things I don't *Like*:
Lumbar punctures' Lightning down my spine.
Lyrica that stops me burning at the stake
but ices my mouth, face, chest, and hands
so I can't feel when I'm burnt or cut.
For *Legions* of cranial *Lesions*
and for *Lead-Lined*, nuclear syringes.

M is for the *Mocking, Murderously* loud
MRI that *Maps* and *Marks*
the *Many* scars in my back and brain
and for *Myokymia,*
my face twitching evenings
just in time for bed.

N is for the *Neurology* ward
where I *Nervously* counted the beds
of MS patients that first week
and wondered why I was there.
For *Neuropathy*, the first sign:
skin tingling as if sunburnt
or being *Nibbled* by insects from inside.

O is for *Optic atrophy* and *neuritis*
seeing sometimes
as through an *Opaque* gauze.
O is also for *Orgasms*
now few and far between.

P is for *Paraplegia*, a weakness in both legs
Paresthesia, pins and needles in hands and feet,
and for the *Plaque* that shorts out my cranial circuits,
for the *Psychologist*, who softens the *Pain*
in my head, or maybe just my head.
For *Placebo* the reason why I won't go experimental.

Q is for *Quadriceps* that cramp in the pool or in bed,
and for *Quadriparesis*, a progressive weakness
in my arms and legs.

R is for *Rectum* and *Relaxation*
both needed for a good shit.
R is also for *Remission* and full *Range* of motion
both I no longer expect.

S is for *Sex, Spasticity,* and *Sphincter* problems,
for *Spinal cord* and *tap* examinations
and for *Symptoms* I quit counting after my *Sixth* year.

T is for the nocturnal *Tremors*,
the bodily earthquakes
that *Toss* me awake
in the middle of the night.

U is for *Urethra* that sometimes
doesn't seem connected to my bladder
and *nUclear* medicine's *Underground* rooms.

V is for *Vertigo*, and for being *Very* careful
when I get up, so I don't fall down.

W is for the *White*-coated doctors
who count the *White* spots
in my brain after every scan.

X is for *X-ray*, where I was sent before MRIs,
and for anti-depressants such as *Xanax*,
that banish thoughts of self-*eXtinction*.

Y is for the thousands of *Yards*
I've walked along hospitals' *Yellow* lines

And finally, Z is for the *Zonked*-out man from *Zeist*
Zigzagging home from the shops
leaning into his *Zimmer frame*.

FIRST SIGNS

FIRST SIGNS

The buzzing in my feet between bed and shower
the trips and falls down the stairs on my way out the door
the earplugs near playgrounds or on buses, trams, or trains
the transit tickets that slipped mysteriously from my grip
the student papers and exams that graded themselves in my filing cabinet
the fourth-year students' names I suddenly forgot in the middle of a lecture
the glass of milk exploding out of my hand at lunch
the knife or fork skidding across my plate
the papers and projects I threw away, meaning to keep
the papers and projects I kept, meaning to throw away
the coins pushed one by one with numb fingers into coffee machines
the exhaustion that stuck me to the sofa every weekend
the ventilation fan's whirring I heard hours after it stopped
the burning weight of a bed sheet resting on my legs.

THE FAMILIAR STRANGER

Her black mustache
was darker than mine at thirteen
and the wiry hairs
on her chin mole
kept me at a distance,
her house always dark,
yellowed window shades
drawn on both sides
against the neighbors.

She only got out of bed
in the late afternoon
and came downstairs
barefoot, in her nightgown,
to sit in a kitchen chair
on the glassed-in back porch,
its warped, moldy, wooden floor
crowded with tomato plants
potted in rusted coffee cans
the window frames outlined
by potato vines, the spuds
half suspended by toothpicks
above water-filled Mason jars
lined up along the windowsill.

"Clothes and shoes hurt too much,"
she complained to her son, Bobby,
my father. He hung his head
when she called his name or begged
for a pill from his drugstore
to put out the fire in her legs.

By my next visit, a year later,
her bed had been moved down
to a room off the kitchen; she was
too weak, too dizzy to climb stairs,
her eyes swimming, mouth twisted,
unsure of me, the familiar stranger.

THESE LEGS

These legs were once my best feature.
For years they carried me everywhere
and, as a high school freshman,
they took me, for three months,
to the top of my class.

How the girls jumped into the pool
that previous summer to pull on
the leg hairs the other boys didn't have.
They grabbed my limbs and tried to pull me under.
I roiled the water and shook them off.

These legs carried me through many dark, wet, frozen
paper-route mornings, my feet tingling from what I thought
was the cold. They were my escape from a table
of bad food and nightly arguments, the burning
in my feet finally gone as I walked miles from home,

through the snow, up a hill overlooking the airport.
I sat on a cold bench and watched the flashing
red, yellow, and green lights of arriving and departing flights,
and counted the years, the months, the days
until I would board one and be gone.

AFTER THE FALL

It's too late to wear a cycling helmet
to install rails and bars in the bath and hall
to use a cane when you get out of bed at 3 A.M.
to use the toilet, to prevent you from hitting
the tile floor that knocks you out,
and blood seeps into your brain.

After the fall, you look like you lost a fight:
face black, blue, and yellow;
nose scraped red; one eye swollen shut.
If you're lucky, you'll get the clot removed
before you forget things, lose your balance forever,
or have trouble mumbling: "Hospital!"

JUST TWO STEPS

Just two steps, I think,
my reason muddled by
weeks of searing pain in my feet
as if I'd just walked barefoot
over a hot, stony, summer beach
and wasn't standing in boots on a cold,
level, concrete station platform
waiting for my last train home.

Just two steps,
this Friday evening after
another sixty-hour work week.
I'm too tired to argue
with this resolution
to my pain and exhaustion:
The first step to clear the raised,
white warning dots, and the second to merge
with the windy, yellow-and-blue rush
of the Maastricht to Groningen Express.

Just two steps.
Gray lines of commuters
flank me, unwilling witnesses.
What will it do to their day
and the rest of their lives
and to the engineer, who'll need to be changed
as a crew collects the pieces of what is left,
and washes the locomotive's bloody nose
before it and everyone can finally roll on?

Just two steps.
if I walk farther up the track
maybe they won't see the impact
but my burning, numb feet
won't carry me that far tonight
so it's here or nowhere.
Just two steps. I close my eyes.

I take one step forward
and one step—

the train blasts past

—back from the edge.
No, not today.
Not this way.

...AND THAT VERY SAME EVENING

"We missed you at the Association's conference.
I don't know if anyone has mentioned this,
but you won the Article of the Year Award.
Please let us know where we can send
your check for the prize money and the plaque."

TODAY I FORGOT

Today I forgot
"funnel," "protractor," and "stethoscope"
for the pictures
on the speech therapist's cards.
"Not to worry," she said,
I still had the vocabulary
of an average man,
no words left—in English or Dutch
to tell her my IQ
was once 138.

Last year my right leg
first did a dance on its own
shaking me awake
in the middle of the night.
Last vacation I pushed
coins across counters,
collected change in
an outstretched palm
to avoid them slipping
through somnolent fingers.
Last month even my sentences
became infected: words missing,
written twice or in the wrong places.

Six medications, one for each year
since the fire first started
after my poem about homophobia
appeared in the church magazine.
The invisible sunburn in my right foot
lit the tinder for the fire that crept up my legs,
flames licking my groin and anus.
Within a month the neurologist's
pin pricks to my posterior
didn't make me jump,
my ticket to the MRI's
banging, narrow, hot, white tunnel

my head in a cage, unable to move
my body fed to the magnetic fire
as William Tyndale for his Bible
Joan of Arc for her male armor
Bruno for his multiplicity of worlds
and I, the faggot heretic,
bound and burning on this plank.

HERE'S SOMETHING FOR THE PAIN

Scan 1

The kindly orderly
told my nervous partner
it would be only 20 minutes
and apologized an hour later
when I was still stuck inside
the noisy, narrow, plastic tube
a second contrast IV in my arm.

Scan 2

At the university hospital
I asked for calm, classical music
to drown out the scanner's metallic,
arrhythmic, robotic orgy.
Instead Mozart's *Requiem*
jeered through headphones
I couldn't switch off or remove,
the control room technician gone
to prepare another patient.

Scan 3

Locked inside the hot, tight
white tunnel, the big magnets'
machine gun mating in my ears
as the MRI scanned,
sliced and mapped my head—
so accustomed
to the hard cushion
of noise and heat,
I started to fall asleep
until the technician shouted:
"Wake up!
You're ruining the results!"

Scan 4

I looked up in the scanner's mirror
and saw the tech and a white-coated doctor
pull up chairs and point at a monitor,
then wave in students from the hall.
They took pictures with their cell phones
and in those flashes I saw myself
five years later, rolling with wheels,
before the doctors even told me
about the scars in my brain.
They tossed me out of hospital that evening:
"There's nothing we can do.
Here's something for the pain."

THE LAW OF THE CONSERVATION OF ANXIETY

My high school English teacher said
I had no insulation, her explanation
why noise and bright light cut through me
when other students didn't jump or blink.

By the time I got to college I believed in
The Law of the Conservation of Anxiety:
Distress is neither created nor destroyed,
but transferred from one body part to another.

And in this law's inertial corollary:
why my body at rest remained at rest
and once in motion, remained frantically in motion
attending lectures, doing homework, writing papers

in the days I could see clearly, walk, and think,
never knowing when stabbing backaches,
headaches, or groin pains would lay me low
on the floor of a dark, cool room.

Now, more than forty years later,
the doctors think they have a formula
for why my body betrayed me:
Genetics + viral trigger + environment = MS.

Genetics: My grandmother's mysterious illness
that kept her upstairs until mid-afternoon,
why clothes and shoes burned her skin
and only pills could quell the pain.

Viral trigger: Scarlet fever's lasting damage my eighteenth summer
my temperature so high in the 90° heat
I sneezed and shivered at the slightest breeze
from the open window at the foot of my bed.

Environment: The weekends and summers
I spent in the library out of the sun

avoiding bullies, not playing ball,
reading every book in the young adult section.

Genetics + viral trigger + environment = MS.
The reason why now I can't
take things off shelves in crowded stores,
or walk a straight line without leaning on a cane.

Why sometimes I go left
when I mean to go right,
or move when I should stop,
trapped in a body that ignores,

twists or garbles my thoughts
fingers that drop or lose tickets
type words twice or leave them out
incredible for the former Head of English

my correspondence once letter-perfect.
Now my computer
reads back what I have written
to spot mistakes my eyes can't.

The reason for the ophthalmologist's
"Hmms," "Ahhhs," and long pauses
when he shined the bright light
through my eyes, revealing their red roots.

My symptoms echoed across the Internet:
a twenty-two-year-old runner misdiagnosed with prostatitis,
who got dizzy, then collapsed at work;
a chat show host with buzzing leg numbness

and the sensation of a hot nail
driven through his penis during sex;
and a temporarily blinded young mother
who needed new glasses when her sight returned.

Genetics + viral trigger + environment = MS.
A conjecture, as in the first years of AIDS,
when "no exchange of bodily fluids"
was the mantra of prevention.

The irony of running for thirty-five years
from one unknown, incurable disease
that killed two dozen friends and two partners
only to be caught by another.

Genetics + viral trigger + environment = MS
more theory than science
as doctors wait for statistical proof
and I, swallowing pain pills, for a cure.

BETHESDA

BETHESDA

I struggle in the dark, narrow booth
jabbing my elbows as I remove my T-shirt
and almost slip off the fold down bench
as I wriggle out of my underpants.

Dressed and showered poolside
I wait with two dozen women,
the only man in the fibromyalgia/MS group,
for the mothers with toddlers to clear out

of the warm, menthol-blue water—
my Bethesda, Hebrew and Aramaic
for both (dis)grace and mercy
as was illness and healing in Jesus' time,

a transgression, a fall from grace.
Bethesda—thought to be a myth
until Schick uncovered the bath
just as written in the Gospel of John:

"Beyond the Sheep's Gate," a pool
with five porticos where the infirm
sat or lay waiting for the angel
to stir the waters, the first one in, healed.

The pool guard removes the floating cord
that separates the shallows from the deep
and the swimmers rush in. I slowly enter
the only water that doffs the fire

inside my feet, legs, back, and groin.
Standing up front, I focus on the instructor,
my movements synchronized with hers,
my earplugs muffling a dozen conversations.

I bend, stretch, step, and as I turn,
look at the pale-yellow winter sun

and thin, white snowflakes tumbling
through evergreen branches.

Bethesda, my weekly ritual,
buoyant in warm water for an hour,
which, unlike the angel's gift,
offers only temporary relief.

DRESS OXFORDS

Twice a week as I grab
my sport shoes for rehab
from the hall closet,
I pause at the shrine
of the man I never was:
the double rack of shiny black and brown
waterproof, leather-soled, dress Oxfords
bought for the long, wet, Dutch winter
that runs from October to April.
Two elegantly thin, B-width pairs
I brought back from America each year.

I planned to wear them in Amsterdam
to the ballet, the theatre, and my dining club,
which I couldn't attend
due to working sixty-hour weeks
to keep my job and a flat.
Even the Nobel Prize winner's reading,
just down the road from college,
I missed because of prep work for class.
Weekends, I was strangely too tired
to get out of my chair or off the sofa
and out the door to catch the bus
to the train to the tram through the rain.

After my "episode," there was no doubt
why I never made it out.
These shoes no longer fit
feet swollen by pills that quell
the tingling, burning, stabbing pains
that begin as soon as toes touch leather.
I stomp around in oversized, double-wide
Frankenstein clogs with tire-tread soles
that grip the ground as I lurch
down the street with my cane.

THE BRACES

They stand in my shoes
at the end of the bed,
the legs I now use
when I travel out of town
on holiday or to the city;
black plastic knee pads
held up by steel rods
fused to metal soles
perfectly balanced
inside a pair of my shoes
standing up on their own.

I've worn them ever since
that afternoon I lost my legs
on Amsterdam's Leidseplein
stranded for half an hour
amidst the jugglers, their
crowds and the pickpockets,
sitting on my rollator
before I thought to walk
sideways the last meters
into a Central Station bound tram.

Hidden braces that protect me
from train passengers who

push and crash to the toilet
or rush to the disabled seats
their luggage smacking
against the plastic pads
instead of my kneecaps
as they hurry past
too busy to stop and say:
"Sorry," which in Dutch
can mean: I'm sorry,
May I get by? or
GET OUT OF THE WAY!

Braces that hold me up
in return for a little pain
from Velcro bindings
that pinch and red-band legs,
the blood trapped underneath,
but which also decrease swelling,
so after a long flight I can still
find my ankles when I finally
undress in my hotel room
and lay down exhausted
from a day of travel
my legs still standing,
waiting at the end of my bed.

SCHWARZWÄLDER KIRSCHTORTE

The young hospital doctor
shuts her office door and switches off her pager.
Her tense face and pinched eyes betray
her forced smile and my good test results
minutes before she gets to what's wrong,
this time, with my brain, heart, or lungs.

Which finally makes me stop thinking
about the Schwarzwälder Kirschtorte revolving
downstairs on the café's mirrored cake carousel,
a gustatory miracle of cherry liqueur,
twin layers of chocolate cake and whipped cream.
I pay more attention and time slows down
while she explains, in Dutch, which part of me
they can't reach or cure this time:
another burnt fuse in my brain that muddies
even my English pronunciation, a heart valve that
won't close completely, or a spot on my lungs,
acquired after a bout with double pneumonia
last summer, that makes my laugh whistle.

I think of that cake and then of my gym-fit friends
thirty years ago, their tanned, muscled bodies
melted down in months to jaundiced skeletons
connected to tubes disappearing into more holes
than God ever gave them,
trying to hang on another week, another month
for a new drug to give them
another week, another month to gasp, choke, and sweat.
I had to take vacation days
to attend their funerals,
so many funerals in so few years,
I put a continent and an ocean
between myself and that place.

I think of those young men and come back to the room,
try to comfort the young doctor who hasn't lost (m)any yet,

tell her I understand my "options," thank her for her time, and go downstairs to eat a piece of that cake.

WINKING THROUGH THE MENTHOL

Twenty minutes in the warm water pool,
halfway through the exercises,
my forehead starts twitching
from pickax strikes behind my right eye.

Unable to speak clearly, I form a T
with my hands for the instructors
and hang with both arms poolside
to wait out this brain storm

set off by too much information,
too many voices echoing off
tiled decks and concrete walls,
my body moving not just forward and back,

but up and down, semi-suspended in space
water splashing against my arms and chest
the pool floor's distorted black lines
waving and winking through the menthol.

I hang there wishing I'd put in my earplugs,
left behind in their plastic case in my locker.
I close my eyes, breathe deeply and wait
for my internal Ramón Mercader to stop striking.

One of the two instructors stands nearby in the water
in case I lose my grip and need to be hauled out.
Five minutes later, my brow smooths, the attack over.
I open my eyes: "I'm back."

GLASGOW MEETING

August 2004

The warden asks if I'd
"rather take the lift?"
"Next time," I say as I lean
into the wooden rail
of the converted, midtown armory's
grand, brown-and-white winding staircase.
Once upstairs in the large room
I sit heavily, wheezing into one
of the many empty chairs
that fill up as meeting gathers.

I close my eyes and remember
Friday's Lake Windermere cruise
Saturday's whitewashed Dove Cottage
and listen to the rainy rush of traffic
on the nearby, elevated M8.
My right leg burns and my ears ring
after a week of 2 A.M. hotel
corridor shouts and door slams.
I think of the strangers
next to me who are Friends
as I center down.

I count my breaths
cleaning up the messy house
that is my mind and body
from the damp, musty basement
to the cluttered, dusty attic
until I feel the warm morning sun
shine through the tall windows
brightening against my closed eyelids:
light, light, more light

LIGHT, LIGHT, MORE LIGHT
my leg no longer burning
my ears no longer ringing

seventy men, women, and children
sitting in silence in the upper room.

THE FIRE FROM ABOVE

Amsterdam, 2010

For six years I was consumed
by tongues of fire, not from above
like the early saints at Pentecost,
but from my feet to my loins.

Flames only pills can put out, singeing, licking
my lower body, a taste of the lake of fire
through which the priests warned I'd wander
that spring I left parochial school

or as my mother predicted would happen
the fall I returned to college with a man.
In minutes she had me on the sidewalk
doubled up in pain at her vision

of my soul engulfed in flames
and her story of how at nineteen she'd driven
down to Texas to see her army boyfriend
and found a suicidal alcoholic, living with his captain.

Now meeting is the only place I can sit for an hour,
where my feet and legs no longer ignite
as I let go of these infernal stories,
waiting for the fire from above.

THE RATTLE

"You're so brave!"
the young woman
from my flight
says as she
catches up with me
at baggage claim and stands
next to my wheelchair.
She watched me wiggle
twice down the airplane's aisle
to the toilet, cane in one hand
the other hand skimming along
the overhead luggage rack.
What's my choice? I think,
but instead I say "Thank you."
She tells me her father
with MS no longer travels.

I'm not brave, just grateful
for the leg braces and walker
that keep me upright,
and for the colorful little pills,
those modern pharmaceutical miracles,
that rattle when inspected by airport security,
that freed me from a hospital bed
and the medicated, carehome nightmares
of my grandmother's last years.

In her memory every Sunday,
more regularly than I attend meeting
I refill my plastic pillbox,
with orange and green Tamsulosin
to plug the leaks in my underpants,
oblong, orange-brown Valsartan
to keep the pipes upstairs from bursting,
white Atenolol to slow
my irregular, frantic heart,
and tiny hydrochlorothiazide,

that slips or jumps through my fingers,
to prevent both grandfathers' fatal strokes.

Not to forget red and white Lyrica
to extinguish the sub-dermal fire,
that starts in my feet the moment I step out of bed
and slowly kisses and licks its way up my legs
until by lunch I'm burning at the stake,
and lastly, green and white Cymbalta
to keep Lyrica's suicidal side-effect fireman
from self-immolating.

Once a week I pop pills from foil packs
into seven plastic compartments
refilling the shaman's magic rattle:
the real courage in my chest,
safely tucked away in my onboard bag.

BURGUNDY

Lunching in the hospital café
I notice the left sleeve
of my dark red T-shirt
suddenly grown longer.
I put on my glasses and see
the white gauze bandage
applied by Phlebotomy
gone a rich, wet burgundy.

The cashier nods and points up
as I ask him to watch my lunch.
He makes change for a customer
without missing a beat,
certainly not the first time one
of his diners has sprung a leak.

Upstairs, I don't have to wait
minutes for the always-on-the-phone
receptionist to finally see me.
She drops the horn and buzzes me right in
and I'm rushed to one of the back booths
with black, padded beds covered
in roll-down, white paper sheets.
The nurse applies a compress
the size of a newborn's diaper
and tells me not to move for thirty minutes.

PRAATGROEP

(literally: talk group; denotation: support group)

It's all so familiar, yet anonymous,
this circle of old, mismatched chairs,
every first Tuesday evening,
just off the hospital corridor:
a room with a worn, stained carpet
furnished with a sofa, two standing lamps
(the overhead fluorescent lights switched off)
a coffee table stocked with magazines,
a tray of clean white cups, spoons, and a cookie tin.
It's supposed to resemble someone's living room.
However, the coffee here is bitter
and the cookies taste like sugar and sand.

Half have lost a partner—
deserted, on average, a year after diagnosis—
or a part of themselves they'll never recover:
the use of an arm, their legs, their vision.
The women complain about pain;
how sex hurts in every position.
One brags about resort and spa holidays,
her summer house in the South of France
and her electric mobility cart
whose beeps and bleeps precede her
seconds before she rolls into the room
and whose curtain of perfume lingers
fifteen minutes after she's gone.
The men talk about job loss
and what they do now:
collecting the grandchildren at school
and taking the dog to the park.

Tonight a thin, bald man says he tastes vanilla
when he stretches his neck to shave.
Another with a beard laments the loss of his car,
dependent now on his wife and the mobility taxi.

A woman, wearing black high heels,
weeps about her removal from her third-floor apartment
without an elevator, to a ground-floor nursing home bed.

I come to listen about new treatments,
avoid the complaints, gossip, coffee, and cookies
cautious, unwilling to reveal to strangers
my anger at being forced out of my job,
and living on half my former salary.
I like the door-to-door taxi
no longer needing to lift my rollator
or wheelchair into a bus or train
without the driver's or a passenger's assistance
or requesting someone to vacate a DISABLED seat.

I refuse the self-injectable trials,
my doctor offering to send
a nurse to my house the first time
to show me how to shoot up,
wary of interferon, which was supposed
to strengthen my friends' weak immune systems
as they died of AIDS in the early '90s,
now offered to stop my over-active white cells
from gnawing on my nerve endings,
afraid also of the chemo/radiation combo
immune system "reboot" on offer,
confined for weeks in a germ-free bubble.

No, I'll keep my vitamins and pills
I can stop if they make me ill
or don't seem to help,
as I wait for a proven cure
unwilling to risk
what little I have left.

WHY I LIKE THE BALLET

There was too much shouting at home
for me ever to enjoy the opera
nor is it easy for me to imagine
two dumpy, middle-aged leads
as Tristan and Isolde.
The Concertgebouw's tight seating
makes my legs burn
even before intermission.
Besides there's nothing to look at
except the conductor
chopping and caressing thin air,
the hall's sixteen-foot, gold organ pipes
as big as God's teeth, or the occasional
violin bow going the wrong direction.

No, the Dutch National Ballet for me!
Its bulimic ballerinas starved to silhouettes—
just heads and hips on which to hang
tiaras and tutus twinkling
with rhinestones and sequins
shimmering in the blue-white spotlight
leaving phosphorescent wakes—
make me forget what they have to do
to get their feet into those toe shoes.

And the muscled, male principals
such as Matthew Golding (what a name!)
one of the troupe's many imports
whose leaps and lifts alone
are worth twice the price of admission.
(Though you wouldn't have recognized him
an hour earlier at warm-ups
in baggy sweats, ashen-faced, matted hair.)
He leaps on to the stage
in a white and gold-roped
marching band top, suddenly tanned.
(They really *can* work miracles in Makeup.)

God's drum major or a leaping lion tamer,
his unruly mane now golden and under control
white tights wrapping bulging buttocks
hard as a horse's hindquarters.
He smiles, then lifts and twirls
yet another ballerina
without grunting or missing a step
his primal, almost naked photo
on the program cover
feet flexed like fists
both legs bent under him in midair
a "Don't try this at home, folks"
stunt showing he's
won his Rite to Spring.

The real reason I go to the ballet:
to feel a little lighter for three hours
before my feet stutter again across
the Stopera's bright lobby.
Into another rainy, windy afternoon
I go, leaning into my cane.

WHY I HATE GENERICS

Five kilos of water retention in two weeks,
blood pressure so high
my heart monitor thumps,
back pains, difficult, burning urination,
sweating, tingling, twitching legs and feet,
pills that taste or smell fishy or moldy,
the sudden dump of non-time released, unbuffered
pavement-lifting relief that lasts a third as long.

Because I know why the Cleveland Clinic runs
its own quality testing lab for its transplant patients' generics
Because I know more about my pills' excipients,
tests, APIs, and bioequivalence than my pharmacist
Because generics are made at rarely inspected plants,
bad batches discovered only by dumpster-diving inspectors
Because I was given a generic blood pressure pill
with a carcinogenic ingredient for over a decade

Because I must explain to my pharmacist,
who's not a chemist and who's never
made medications from scratch—
run tar titrations for dandruff shampoos all weekend,
prepared ingredients to one-tenth of a gram,
slathered lanolin and glycerin on marble plates
with a blunt knife to make custom eczema creams
as my father did in his pharmacy lab—
why cheap drugs can't be the same
as those four times as expensive
Because most of the time
you *do* get what you pay for.

MORNING EXERCISES

Bicycle on your back in bed
until you're more tired
than from the horizontal mambo
(naturally, no longer on top).

Still on your back:
Stretch your legs
straight up along the wall,
then swivel them sideways and down.
Crawl the wall
with your hands to sit up,
slide and wiggle on a board
from bed to wheelchair.

Roll down the hall to the loo,
tip back to go over the door lintel,
transfer from the chair, spinning
like a gymnast, hands on the armrests,
to the parallel bars along the toilet.
Read a book whilst
your colon slowly remembers
what it's supposed to do.
In the mirror, after shaving
flex your cheek muscles
into a slight grin until they hurt
to smooth out an old man's scowl.

Decide you're not too tired to make breakfast
swallow your morning meds with yogurt.
Toss the wheelchair over your shoulder into the trunk
slide against the side of the car then pivot
like a fashion model in a short skirt
into the driver's seat.

FALL TRAINING

You unlock the big, blue, gymnastics mat
from the wall and let it slam to the floor
so we can practice how to fall.

You fall backward: twist and roll,
draining the energy that can break bones,
your feet, legs, and buttocks up in the air.

You fall sideways: your T-shirt lifts
from your waistband to reveal
the same tan as on your face and hands.

You fall forward: you head-tuck,
crumple, and roll twice. You ask
if I'd like to practice these moves again.

I shake my head, unable to speak
draw quick circles with my hand
to indicate I've lost my balance

not knowing if I can hold
everything in or down if I fall again
after you onto that soft rubber mat.

THIS HOUSE OF DISABLED PEOPLE

It's clean and quiet here, no one runs and shouts
down halls with orange sherbet walls,
blueberry chairs, lemon window frames,
and lime picnic tables and benches.

Here patients in wheelchairs or walkers,
who wear new, blue, customized
plaster casts and skull caps,
wheel outside to re-indulge in bad habits

after a stroke, episode, or heart attack,
a motorcycle or automobile accident.
Some may never speak, walk, ride, or drive again
but most can still hold a cigarette or a smuggled drink.

The first week they get by on false courage
to meet their complete, well-scrubbed families
who visit with hopeful bouquets, and who,
by the second, have learned to phone ahead

to avoid flying meal trays and drinks
thrown in tirades and tears
by those who've just heard they must
permanently exchange legs for wheels.

My neurologist hesitated to send me here
afraid I'd be disturbed by pool amputees,
but here among the wheelchairs and toilets,
with grab bars and emergency cords, I feel safe.

My previous hydrotherapy group met at a public pool,
its disabled changing carrels taken by parents with infants
or shouting school children slamming metal locker doors,
dirty diapers and smashed French fries left behind on the floor.

Here, in this pool, I listen to the water splash against my chest
talk quietly with the other patients about gardens and pets,

and rarely about the "procedures" that absent us
the weeks our wounds must stay dry to heal.

Here it's quiet and clean, no one runs or shouts
no matter how many times I need to take a break
along the pool's rim. In this house of disabled people,
for three hours a week, I feel able and complete.

PATIENT SAYS "NO"

PATIENT SAYS "NO"

While he's got me on my knees,
up on that special, padded lift
that puts my rectum at eye-level
the proctologist suggests

a shot of Botox in my bum
to release my tight "Oh!" rings,
"lucky," he says, my appointment was the day
of his once-a-month clinic.

I decline his "special offer"
not wanting a loose caboose
or what my friends refer to as SAS—
saggy ass syndrome.

He's the third specialist
in as many months
I've surprised by saying "No."
The first, a neurologist

who suggested interferon
to suppress my hyperactive
white cells from gnawing on
my nattering nerve endings

even though last winter
I caught every cold
and had the flu twice
despite my yearly jab.

The second, a cardiologist,
who didn't see anything wrong,
yet ordered another nuclear stress test
in the hospital's lead-lined basement

with chemically induced exhaustion
(and hypoxia and nausea the first time)

my legs too weak to break a sweat
on the exercise cycle—and now this!

I feel like Little Britain's
drag hospital receptionist,
refusing everyone's request
with: "Computer says: 'No'"

so she can go off to lunch.
Which is exactly what I do:
say, "No, I don't think so,"
and tell him to put me down.

DON'T ASK

Don't ask around the table
after hydrotherapy, even softly,
about the photos of those
in the attendance book
who no longer come.

Don't ask about the ones who
first walked unaided, next with a cane,
then with a walker, and finally were rolled
in a wheelchair to the pool's edge
and lifted by crane in a sling
in and out of the warm water.

Don't ask about the tall, thin, bald man,
who flew to Montenegro for a spa cure,
had a stroke and never returned,
or the well-traveled women, who wore
their gold necklaces, rings, and earrings
or horn-rimmed glasses into the pool,
before they sailed away on their last cruises.

Don't mention the woman
with the curly, white hair
whose dentures clicked
as she scolded me for not going
to the physical therapy gym
just around the corner from my flat,
who had a stroke and was taken
by ambulance to hospital
eighty kilometers away.

Just as World War II pilots and their crews,
enjoying a warm, mess hall meal,
never mentioned absent aviators
or their own survival odds,
don't ask about those,
whose photos are still in the book,
but no longer around the table.

SIDE EFFECTS

One in ten may experience
the following side effects:
dry mouth, sore throat,
disorientation, irritation,
clumsiness, dizziness, falling,
sleepiness, sleeplessness, exhaustion,
tingling, or a loss of feeling,
equilibrium, erection, or memory loss,
weight gain, muscle cramps, convulsions,
constipation, diarrhea, nausea, flatulence,
joint pain, back pain, arm and leg pain,
speech and gait disorders,
blurred vision, double vision,
swelling of appendages,
suicidal ideation.

WHY I HAVE FIRED MY THERAPISTS

You told my mother, at a joint session, you didn't think I was gay.
You put me on Haldol after I felt my father's passing thousands of miles
     away.
You wouldn't give me anything to calm my hands that shook.
You recommended I buy your self-published, anal pleasure book.
You said not to contact my family—they should have been looking for me!
Your answering machine kept interrupting our guided imagery.
You started snoring towards the end of every session.
You advised me to sleep with someone, as you had, to get a university
     position.
You suggested I steal copy paper from a college that never paid on time.
Your supervisor phoned me, to give you another chance, while you listened
     on another line.
You offered to set me up with another patient on a date.
You couldn't help me with my ill and violent flatmate.
You instructed me to stuff a towel in my mouth and shout.
You declared me "cured" when my insurance ran out.
You kept rescheduling and finally didn't show up.
You shouted, during our last session, for *me* to shut up.
You kept a revolver in your top drawer next to your pad and pen.
When I fired you, you said I'd be back again.

WHAT TV TAUGHT ME ABOUT MS

(And My Doctors Never Mentioned)

From Montel Williams's talk show and book
why sex felt like a hot nail driven through my penis,
why cold weather, snow, and ice-skating
numbed the pain in my feet and legs
and how I got MS from a week-long,
high fever the summer I was seventeen.

From *Oprah* I learned about
abdominal injections of interferon,
from the BBC's *Panorama*,
about an experimental chemo/radiation combination
to reboot my haywire immune system,
from *House* the cause of the night terrors
that kept me single for years,
bolting upright in bed

alone or screaming next to a man
I'd known for months or just met,
walking out the front door
the next morning to the neighbors' stares,
scratches and bruises on my arms and legs,
unable to remember anything,
but feeling strangely calm and rested.

YET ANOTHER CURE

The evening newscaster announces
yet another MS breakthrough:
a 30,000 euro annual infusion
available just over the border
in private clinics, not in hospitals,
nor covered by insurance.

I read past the on-line PR,
about the millions spent
in research, production, and distribution,
and finally find the clinical results:
the new drug helps only thirty to forty percent.
Buried at the bottom, in a footnote:
twenty-one deaths.
I decide again to wait it out.

THE OBJECT OF THEIR LESSON

"Dr. X, cardiologist," he says
as I'm rolled into the OR on a gurney.
"Dr. Monte, anthropologist," I reply.
He shakes my hand, then locks it in a stirrup.

He asks if I'm familiar with "the procedure."
I tell him about the transfemoral I had twelve years ago,
a glue gun at the ready to seal an extra vein
possibly pressing against my spine,
suspected as the cause of my weak, burning legs,
(a year before my MS diagnosis),
a twenty-kilo sandbag placed on my abdomen
and eight hours flat on my back to prevent the plug
from popping out, my groin blue, black, yellow,
red, green, and tender for three months.

He assures me this transradial approach
will be less painful, invasive, and colorful,
administers a local, waits a few minutes,
then punches a small, hot hole in my right wrist.
A group of third and fourth year
students, all in green V-necked scrubs, attend.
As he threads the catheter up my arm
he questions them about the wire gauge
and the best route to my heart. "Over the shoulder,
down the neck, and into the chest," one answers.

He questions over an intercom
the first and second years
who watch from an observation room
about the location and type of blockage,
where and how much to inflate the balloon,
and the number of stents I'll need.
Voices estimate between one and five
as the probe winds through spidery veins
on the surgeon's monitor.

He nods occasionally for an assistant
to sop up my hand's hot wetness.
He asks if I want to look
at the monitor as he places two stents.
I decline, "I'd rather just listen,"
not wanting to witness a possible wrong turn
or perforation while the wire's still in me.

Within minutes, the line is reeled back,
a small, plastic, pillbox air bandage placed
on my wrist to reduce bruising.
I ask the surgeon if I have another ten years.
He says, "You can live to a hundred if you want."
(My father dead from his fourth coronary at my age),
I'm happy to hear this and to be
in a university lecture hall again
filled with curious, bright, eager students
even if I am the object of their lesson.

ON THE LEVEL

ON THE LEVEL

I struggle to stay upright on the platform
leaning against the side of the train
at Utrecht Central Station, pushed and jostled
from behind as I swing my rig up two steps.
No one offers assistance.
Passengers stream and squeeze past,
then take the disabled seats
next to the entrance, their eyes glazing over,
staring off into space as I roll up,
their bottoms covering the pictograms
of canes and wheelchairs printed
into the upholstery, their backs to
the blue and white signs
posted above their heads.
I say: *Goede morgen, middag,* or *avond*
and ask for a volunteer to yield a seat:
their blunt, blank stares turn to icy daggers.

At the airport of "America's most unfriendly city"
the wheelchair attendants argue
about who is going to push "him!"
to and through security,
as if I cannot hear them,
when they are standing just a few feet away.
The loser starts pushing me slowly
to the wrong end of the terminal.
I protest, so I don't miss my flight,
my comfort in the hands of a hostile stranger;
I think *no tip* and thank God
for those thin pieces of plastic
in my wallet, and the meet and greet
chauffeur numbers programmed into my cell phone,
in case I do miss a flight and need to stay the night,
since now I must roll everywhere I go
just to keep things on the level.

NO ONE EVER ASKS

I only attend once a month
when my allotted cab ride
takes me and my wheelchair
fifty kilometers north.
When traffic is light I arrive
early and wait on the sidewalk
at the foot of four steps
that lead to a locked door.

I will come as long as
my arms can lift
my chair and my bottom
up one step at a time.
The toilet's another challenge
too narrow for my wheels
I walk the walls with my hands
and leave the door unlocked.

After meeting, someone
usually brings me a coffee
when I take out my pills
but no one ever asks
why I never stay for lunch
or monthly business meeting
both up the long, steep staircase
to the second floor.

NOBODY

The name Odysseus gave Polyphemus
to outwit and escape the "rude and lawless" Cyclops
as he planned his escape from the giant's cave
with at least some plunder and half his crew after
the giant had boulder-blocked their exit and eaten six men,
violating his divine obligation to hospitality.
"Who did this to you?" the other one-eyed giants asked
summoned by Polyphemus' blinding screams.
And he gave them the name Odysseus gave as his own:
"Nobody is killing me," which one professor
said Homer meant as comic relief, while others
claimed the giants augured Polyphemus' pain
as divine punishment, so none offered assistance,
and Odysseus and his crew escaped to their ship.

"Nobody ever uses this ramp," the bus driver says
as she reluctantly gets her hook to pry up
and open the folded metal ramp encrusted
with a year's dirt to the bus's floor.
"Nobody ever uses this toilet,"
the concierge says as she leads me through
a warren of passages in the modern building
and asks if I can make it up "just two steps."
"Nobody has ever graduated in a wheelchair,"
the beadle says the day I receive my PhD,
his office down a spiral staircase with no lift.
All three use a referent that erases my presence.
Unlike Odysseus, I give none of them my name,
hoping to navigate safely the dangerous way home.

THERE IS A DIFFERENCE

I'm that somewhat unpleasant reminder
that in every public convenience, vehicle, or building
there should always be a way for me
to get up and down stairs
without getting out of my chair
and a place to park and clamp my rig
before the bus, tram, or train moves.

A button next to the door
to let myself into buildings
and a way to let the bus driver know
I'm waiting where others
are exiting, just in case
I don't register in the mirror.

I need pushbutton ramps and lifts
so I'm not expected to back-flip
the gap between bus and curb.
I'm no stuntman, so sometimes
I use humor with drivers
who grunt, set the brake
and grumble as they get out of their seat
to manually fold out the ramp
with a hook to the sidewalk
while I sing: *"Vouw uit de helling,*   (Unfold the ramp
de helling, de helling uitvouwen"   the ramp, the ramp, unfold)
as if I were at Oktoberfest,
making some riders smile
but also warning the mothers on board
with baby buggies stuffed with shopping,
in the yellow phosphorescent square
emblazoned with a wheelchair logo,
not just to stand there and glare
but to move with their children into the coach,
so I don't have to wait in the rain
for the next bus and miss my train.

There is a difference between being tired
and being disabled, between being pregnant
and being disabled, between being a mother
with young children and being disabled.
I would gladly use the front door and stand
for you, if I could, but I can't, so you should.

GRAVITY

The force that keeps my wheels
fixed to the pavement
pulls me down ramps
as I'm offloaded from a bus,
then suddenly flips me
as a passerby's boot
blocks my front wheel
and I'm pitched forward, my head
striking the bus stop's metal bench.

The force that pulls down
the expectant smiles of friends
I haven't seen in years,
their spontaneous jaw drops
as I'm rolled into arrival halls
after a long flight, as they scan
the crowd at head-height
for my narrow, angular face
and thick, brown hair,
as they finally look down
and see a moonfaced man
with thinner, salt and pepper hair,
legs braced by foot pads,
pushed by a wheelchair attendant.

The force that makes
these faces stumble,
mouths open in a circle,
and bodies bend down as if to greet
a child and not a man,
pulled by a sudden gravity.

INERTIA

is what keeps me going
left, right, left, right, left.
I put one foot or hand in front of the other
just as Frans Biberkopf, a murderer,
did upon release from Weimer Berlin's Tegel prison,
to steady his overloaded head filled with the noise
of rushing electric trams stuffed with people
and tall buildings that seemed
about to tumble down and bury him,
as he tried to go straight in that crooked city.

Inertia is what keeps me seated
when I should stand up, silent
when I should speak out, on the days
I can't walk, and cab and bus drivers
jerk me around in my chair.
One even broke off a front wheel
and set me stranded on a sidewalk,
a hundred meters from home.
"It just fell off," he said.

Left, right, left, right, left, is what I must think
on the days my legs barely work
leaning heavily into my rollator,
my neural network no longer on autopilot
each step by special request to my short-circuited brain.
I try to cover the three hundred meters to the post office.
Another three hundred to physical therapy
is out of the question, if I want to return home.

I was an object in motion that stayed in motion
my last two and a half years at the private university
rushing out the door of my last lecture to catch the bus
to the train to another city to the twice-weekly night school
to pass the four-part, two-day national exam
to get the language and culture diploma
to land the sixty-hour-a-week public college

headteacher's job I kept for over a decade
for the forty hours-a-week pay, always rushing
to finish grading the endless stacks of projects, papers
and exams that kept me busy nights, weekends, and holidays
so I didn't notice I had no time for friends or vacations
or I forgot what I'd wanted to visit
when I'd first moved to Europe,
until one day
a mist of exhaustion enveloped me
and I collapsed in the street, unable to speak.

Left, right, left, right, left,
I measure out steps
and handholds every morning
as I walk down the hall,
holding onto a wall or a rail
to wherever it is I'm going.

THE ROTOR

A morning shower earns me a free ride
on The Rotor as I sit up on my bed
my back stuck against the cool, concrete wall;
the room spins and the floor drops away.

If I close my eyes, I become nauseous,
the room turning even faster.
The only distance I will travel today
is between bed and living room couch.

The radio plays
a Gershwin rhapsody:
glissando piano runs and whinnying clarinets
pinging my head and spine.

THE MASK

snaps itself into place
just in time for sleep:
cheeks and jaws taut
facial muscles locked
so tight that massage,
deep-breathing, aspirin,
paracetamol, or another pregabalin
can't loosen it.

At 1 A.M. I finally
take an ibuprofen
that can raise
my blood pressure,
make my temples throb
or my back ache,
but I will get no sleep
if I don't self-medicate.

No one knows the mask-maker,
but as usual with MS
there's no end of suspects:
eating, shaving, talking,
a light breeze,
tooth brushing, face washing,
drinking, air conditioning,
vibrations from walking
or bus or car travel,
smiling, kissing, loud sounds,
or sudden head movements,
anything you'd do before,
during, or after your average date,
not that I've gone out for years.

The late-night newscasters
lose their second set of eyes,
and the rictus slowly releases
as the ibuprofen does its work.

THE HUG

My chest is suddenly compressed
as if hugged by an obnoxious uncle,
who holds on too long
or squeezes too hard
to show off his love or strength,
from whom I fight to get away.

Unexplained spasms
of my intercostal muscles
convulse to create this bear hug.
Claws sunk between my ribs
make it difficult to breathe,
hard to lie down,
impossible to sleep.

The MS website suggests
how to make it release:
wear loose or tight clothes
a hat or no socks
drink hot or cold water
breathe deeply, do yoga,
read, sing, or paint.
It even collects tips
on "How You Manage It."

THE PLUG

For years I felt like a freak
until a guy in my MS support group
complained he too had to remove his shoes,
trousers, and underpants just to take a crap,
the same experience as this cowboy,
who regularly rides the commode in reverse
naked from the waist down
just to push something out.

I was relieved to find out it was
due to a medical phenomena
nicknamed the MS plug, a backup
of waste that doesn't move quickly or
rhythmically enough through my colon
before it hardens and cements itself to my guts.

Since then I've tried
bran,
oats,
walking,
prunes,
dried apricots,
swimming,
cereals,
nuts,
stationary cycling,
even a regular "bathroom time,"
but everything has remained
steadfastly stuck in place
due to the MS plug.

THE HOTEL READING

No! This can't be it! I think as I see
the white, spray-painted wheelchair logo
on the hotel's black brick wall
in the back by the loading dock
just below a camera and a speaker.
But then I remember I live in a land
where lifts and ramps are optional
at historic, public front entrances,
where wheelchairs are still loaded like freight
onto trains never level with platforms,
pushed up or down metal ramps by porters,
who must be requested hours in advance.

I push the button. A man asks
who I am and what my business is.
I tell him I've come to read
for a group on the fourth floor.
He's never heard of them,
but he'll send someone to let me in.

A minute later a cook in a white apron
appears on the loading dock
holding a silver remote control.
He lowers the metal lift to street height
so I can roll in. As I reach out
to push the UP button he says,
"No. Don't touch. I control everything
with this," waving the remote.

From the loading dock
he rolls me into a supply room
stacked with brown cardboard boxes
and white china bowls, plates, and cups
then past the kitchen's steaming
pots and pans, blue gas jets at eye level.
I think, for a second,
of Billie Holiday in the '50s—

before my front wheels stop dead
against a raised doorway lintel.
My bag catapults out of my lap,
thudding onto a hard tile floor,
and I levitate from my chair
standing momentarily weightless
on the footrests.
Just before the point of no return,
I grab the armrests and pull myself
down into the seat again.

Inside the hotel lobby
there's no one in reception to greet me
or to direct me upstairs to the room
where I am to read. I call the number
on my cell phone from the email invitation.
A woman comes down and leads me
to the elevator and then to a hot room
on the top floor, a balcony bar.
I unpack at the front table
and discover two dented spines
in the ten books I've brought to sign.
Better these than mine, I think,
too shaken and hot to bother
about what or how well I will read.

WHILE WE'RE ALL STILL HERE

On my way from the writers' conference dining hall
the first evening, I'm so happy to see Nonnie again
I do a spontaneous back-flip out of my wheelchair
and onto the boardwalk that leads to our rooms.

Nonnie screams, but not with glee.
"Bryan, are you all right?"
"Never better," I answer.
I crawl back up without a scratch

and wake up the next morning without a bruise.
At breakfast we see Dianne and Magda
drinking coffee, the Fantastic Four from last year's
poet laureate's class now complete.

And the next evening
as a fiction writer's sexy bass voice tells a story
about three teenage casualties at a survival camp
(two of the injured airlifted out),

Dianne shows me two photos on her camera
of her county courthouse's Victorian spire,
and autumn foliage taken through a screen window
and I say: "Hello, summer and autumn issues!"

always looking for pieces for my journal,
as is Magda, a magazine intern in the last cabin
next to the parking lot with her barking dogs,
who asks if she can submit to her magazine,

my abecedarian poem about how I'm falling apart.
I quickly decide she can have it
while I'm still here, while we're all still here
the poet laureate's "mature" students from last year.

SUSPENDED

"One hundred and eight euros, are they worth it?"
the woman who sold me my wheelchair without them
asks as I buy the anti-tip safety wheels
recommended by my rehabilitation therapist

after I was twice tossed out of my chair
onto Milan's concrete subway platforms
performing the double, backwards roll
I couldn't do for an A in high school.

How much does a cracked skull cost? I think.
A few months later these little wheels
catch me in midair as I back out of a train
at Madison Square Garden, tipped at an angle,

suspended between train and platform,
as if a Ferris wheel suddenly stopped turning.
A flurry of passengers' hands sets me gently
on the platform, and then are gone.

WHY I DIDN'T USE THE BACK DOOR

Ga chunk, ga chunk, ga chunk, ga chunk.
I force my wheelchair backwards up the four, broad steps
Of my hometown library's seventeen-million-dollar extension
built with no ramps to allow me to roll through the front door.
The new building's straight-up-and-down, three-story pillars
reminiscent of the *Mussolini Dux* obelisk or EUR's colonnades.

Gone is the old side entrance I used as a child
with a bike rack next to the young people's section,
a sunny, western bay window with a built-in bench.
Now a postmodern entrance hall whisks
unknowing visitors and the homeless from the front door
right out the back before they enter the library.
No information or circulation desk in this great corridor
nor books on a revolving wire rack, as in my day,
          enticing them to stay.

No, this is a library for people who know
where they are supposed to go,
who drive and park out back
who know how to walk left and take
the stairs, or the elevator if they're tired,
to where the books and videos are kept.

Ga chunk, ga chunk, ga chunk, ga chunk.
I roll up to the front counter and ask:
"Why is there no ramp for the front entrance?"
The librarian glares down and informs me of
the two, blue, wheelchair IN REAR logo signs out front.
I tell her a bicycle parked in the rack in front of a car
with its hood over the sidewalk blocked that way in,
and that the days of minorities using the back door are over.
I tell her my family had a business in this town
for twenty-five years, and a house for fifty-two,
and that tomorrow I will call the mayor
and the councilperson responsible for this ward.
She gives me a business card with the name
and contact information of a library administrator.

I take the elevator upstairs and look on the shelves
for a copy of J. P. MacLean's *Shakers of Ohio,*
but it's not where I found it four years ago,
the section since moved over a few rows.
As I roll down the narrow aisles, picking up
discarded stepstools blocking my way with my left foot
and depositing them in the wide aisles at each end,
I hear "Nonfiction" over the loudspeaker,
realize that's where I am.
I hear the policeman's squawk box
a few seconds before he appears—
military-short blond hair and pudgy.
I say: "I'm disabled, not a criminal,"
squint for his badge number and
give him my *Herr Doktor Professor* stare
over my black reading glasses,
so he just walks by with a smirk.
Barely in his 30s, he realizes I can take him
to court or get a comment permanently placed
on his record if he stops, cautions, or arrests me.

Ga chunk, ga chunk, ga chunk, ga chunk.
I wheel to Reference to check for the book
in the on-line card catalogue, every terminal
blocked by a heavy, wooden chair.
I push one out of the way with a grunt
as the phone rings behind me.
The librarian answers: "Yes" meaning, I'm there.
then comes over too late and offers
to move the chair I've already shifted.
I ask why there's no accessible terminal.
She doesn't answer, but asks
which book I am looking for.
I tell her, she checks the number, and we
look for it on the shelf back where I was,
then she checks the number again
and says it was charged out and just returned,

but is downstairs waiting to be re-shelved.
I tell her I'd like to look at it to check
some rare photos I'd just examined
at the Shaker Heights Museum a few days ago,
that I'll be delivering a history paper
in Salt Lake City at the end of the week.
She says the book will be on the shelf tomorrow.
I tell her I will be at the airport then.
She makes no effort to go or call downstairs
to get the book so I can consult it before I go.

Ga chunk, ga chunk, ga chunk, ga chunk.
Sometimes I've wondered why I left
four decades ago to save my family
damage to their name and pharmacy.
Now, in the one place that once offered
my only solace, information, and protection
to do homework, free from bullies
and my parents' nightly arguments,
I know I will never return,
the store long torn down,
a parking lot in its place
a five-story American flag
painted on the wall of the building
still standing next door.

YOUR WHEELCHAIR IS TOO WIDE

There's a reason I always travel
with a tape measure and a camera:
to document "invisible" barriers
like steps or narrow entrances
when I visit public buildings.

Like the museum where I'd
just delivered a conference paper
and where I wanted to buy some postcards
of Revolutionary-era pewter ware,
Amish quilts, and a Benjamin West
Founding Fathers painting magnet

where the store manager told me
my wheelchair was too wide
for the 1950s-era lobby lift
next to the staircase.
I had just barely slipped
through the front entrance
scraping my knuckles
on the door frame.

I told him I'd tried
to use the side disabled entrance
rolled up its leaf and acorn strewn
concrete ramp whose dirty handrails
blackened my hands.
No one was behind the counter
opposite the locked glass door
to hear my knock and let me in.
So I'd come back around
to the front for assistance.

So it's outside again
and up the filthy ramp
where now someone
waits, holding the door open.

Sweating and panting,
I buy my postcards and magnets,
photograph and measure
the doorways and ramp,
and keep my receipt.

YELLOW-RED-BLUE

After Wassily Kandinsky's painting, Gelb–Rot–Blau

"What's it like to have MS?"
On good days, I'm the bright man on the left
able to see and think clearly, riding blue,
yellow, green, and violet auric wakes,
though if I'm outside for more than half an hour,
a hot summer sun's long, thin, sharp pins
can strike and stick in my skull, slur my speech,
and drive a red dagger into my head.

On bad days, I'm the man on the right,
a burgundy silhouette wearing a black visor
and a blue suit, my mind skating
along two lines—one curling, one straight—
that end in or around a deep blue hole.
If I walk without a cane or rollator,
I sway like a drunk, skim walls, graze doorframes.
Passwords, people's names,
what I wanted to do on my computer
are all locked away in scrambled Rubik's cubes.

On these days, it's best
to step away from my desk,
and rest before I delete
or wreck the ineffable yellow, green,
red, blue, and violet vistas
I may never recreate nor remember.

A DRIVE WITH MONDRIAN

Rolling down the A2 on my way
home from another retrospective
at Amsterdam's Stedelijk Museum
I wonder why you abandoned
your realistic green and brown farmyards
for your burgundy, yellow, and blue
cross-hatched impressionist windmills,
and then the bare, bent cubist trees
with angular black and silver branches
for those obsessive black grids
filled with rectangles of white,
gray, blue, yellow, and red.

Was it because you had to leave France
during the First World War
that you renounced cubism
and reduced your palette
for your own constructivism?
Was it the flat Dutch fields
bordered by regularly spaced canals
that made you enclose everything
within black grids, your style,
the signature you took
back to Paris and into other exiles
in London, and then Manhattan
where you died, a septuagenarian pasting
color cut-outs on bare studio walls?

Why so few colors
bounded by black lines?
Was it restful? Did it help
you forget those wild years,
waiting out the first war?
Was it an attempt to make a name
among De Stijl's artists, or to find
the peace and order you sought
in Blavatsky's or Steiner's societies,

or did you just copy van Doesburg's
circa 1918 stained-glass window plan?
I ask myself, strapped into my wheelchair
inside an intercity, disabled cab
traveling 100 kph down the motorway
passing cars of the same six colors:

black
        white   gray
                blue
yellow
     red

rolling down the A2's asphalt lanes.

HOMECOMING

HOMECOMING

*On finding my great-great-grandfather's grave
in Lisanza, Italy*

I missed your headstone that first noon,
its worn engraving stained by frost roses
encrusted with furry yellow-green lichen,
the short, soft, gray vertical marker
wedged into a thin, middle column
of single graves for single men or widowers
who died decades after their wives,
bordered by larger family and matrimonial plots,
covered with horizontal, polished pink or gray marble slabs
as big as double beds with round, stone bolsters.
The blazing, blinding sun pounded my head
as daredevil, little gray-green lizards dived
under tombstones or into the cool brush,
my wheels crunching down white gravel aisles.

Now on a cooler, overcast morning
looking from another angle, I recognize your name
below a worn angel etched in stone
its bowed head resting in its left hand,
its right hand on a headstone within your own.
I rub your name, your *nato* and *morto* with wax onto paper,
then photograph the shadowy inscription
to obtain a copy of your death certificate
at the town hall down the road
to send to my American cousins.

Outside the cemetery gate, the road north
has a view of the snowy Alps.
To the west, Lago Maggiore laps
lazily at the village's private beach
where a tanned, thin, middle-aged couple
sunbathe during their two-hour, midday *riposo*.
I sit in the shade in the town square's café,
drink a frothy coffee, eat a sweet and tart

lemon chicken and avocado sandwich,
feel a cool, lake breeze caress my face
and finally know where I will rest.

FIRST COUSINS ONCE REMOVED

According to my genealogy guide
first cousins once removed share only 6.25% DNA,
but our pillboxes are almost identical;
we compare them in your car
on our drive past the coal mines
where our grandfathers once worked.
You point out dozens of narrow slits
in hillsides spread over just three miles
where miners rode low carts down into the earth
where they lay face up as black rock and dust
rained down all day long in the near dark.

Sulfur Creek still runs through town,
punks the evening air, and at flood,
sullies local wells. You were class valedictorian
as was my dad and his next youngest cousin,
three in one family; even in a small town,
what were the odds of that?
Our grandparents' and great-uncle's
lives shortened by a generation, unlike their
Lago Maggiore fisher/farmer ancestors
who lived into their eighties or nineties.
No one else to take
the dangerous work
the long hours, the low pay,
the moldy housing and food
from the mine owners
and the company store,
how many immigrants
have lived and died
in their new countries.

MOONFACED MAN

Good-bye, rent-controlled
two-story, fourth and fifth floor apartment
with no elevator, overlooking the quiet park.
Good-bye, stepladder, high shelves,
cabinets, counters, and sinks.
Good-bye, upstairs bathroom
and downstairs toilet
and the spiral staircase
that connected them both.
Good-bye, high ceilings
and big windows that
always let the light in.
Good-bye, thin man dressed
in sleek shoes and suits.

Hello, elevator next to the front door
of a condo 20,000 euros underwater.
Hello, everything on one floor,
sinks and cabinets at the right height,
wheelchair-wide hallways,
and a drive-in shower.
Hello, doctors just around the corner
and decades-older, gossipy neighbors.
Hello, low ceilings and heating bills,
smaller windows, darker rooms,
and the river rush of ventilators and unseen traffic.
Welcome home, moonfaced man in the mirror,
whose too-tight clothes and shoes
finally joined the Salvation Army.

SOMEWHERE UNDER THEIR RADAR

I thought that after my call
when you discovered I was still alive
after three and a half years of silence
you'd respect the fidelity and dignity
of my six-year partnership
after I'd forgiven you for forbidding me
to come home after my second partner
was hospitalized a second time with AIDS,
or a decade later, to look for a condo in town.

When I finally came to visit with a partner,
however, you put us in separate beds
in separate rooms, on separate floors,
no family get together, everyone too busy
with jobs and kids to come and meet us
after we'd traveled all the way from Europe,
not even a sheet cake with "Welcome Home"
in icing from the bakery down the street.
Just as a cousin said at my dad's funeral in '88
you were always tight-lipped about what I was doing
out in California, as if I were sitting in prison
and not on Berkeley's dean's list every quarter.

In that last, long decade before you
and your World War II-era neighbors—
who called from their porches
the first time I walked down the street
with my partner, curious to know where I'd been
all those years, and the next day
snapped their doors shut as we passed—
died, and the law finally changed.

Now we're too old for a house with a yard
and children. We take care of ourselves
without anyone's help, as we always have:
one of us underemployed, the other disabled,

in our senior condo with an elevator at the door
exhausted from four decades of living
somewhere under their radar.

TRENTO

Oh, Trento, the Italian strudel capital!
How could I not love you
and your marble sidewalks
in the old town center
over which my wheelchair
rolls almost effortlessly,
your statute of Dante
with his hand thrust forward,
a demonic dragon at his feet,
keeping order in the park
through which I rolled
downhill from the train station
into the Grand Hotel's lobby
with its faux medieval knight
and saint statues standing in reception
and its black and white swirling
Art Deco marble floors guiding
me first to the elevators and then
to a room with a mountain view?

Why did it take so long
for us to meet?
Forty-two kilometers south of
my great-grandfather Donati's home in
Banco with its fin-de-siècle Hapsburg
mayor and church muralist,
post-World War II fireman and priest
bearing my ancestors' names,
your apple trees heavy
with green and red fruit
ready for the picking.

FOR WHOM WE ARE BORN

Non nobis solum nati sumus.
(Not for ourselves alone are we born.)
—from *De Officiis (The Duties)*, by Cicero

At Trento's Catholic Cultural Centre
mesmerized by flickering microfilm
and illuminated, millennium-old books
resting on blue pillows in vitrines,
I search the records trying to trace
my father's mother's mother's lineage
back to her ancestral village.

A young clerk, a college intern,
assists me setting up my carrel,
brings the old village *nati*,
matrimoni, and *morti* books
bound in orange-yellow leather,
their pages filled with small, brown,
faded, practically indecipherable script.

As I show her my family tree
with its bald spots and empty
upper branches, she mentions
her great-uncle's disappearance
after his migration to the U.S.
Her grandfather still wonders
what happened to his oldest uncle:
where he went, why he never wrote,
whether his life was long or short.
I ask for her great uncle's information
his surname, with a distinctive
twist of two final letters,
and an approximate birth date
making a vague promise to assist.

That night at my hotel, before dinner
I check the U.S. census and military records

and *Find a Grave.* Within a half hour
I have a 1940 Pittsburgh address
for an unmarried, thirty-eight-year-old boarder,
a coal miner, who enlisted
in the Marines in '42 and served
four years as a private in the Pacific,
who, after the war, became a steelworker
and died at seventy of a heart attack.

After dinner, I find the ship's manifest
for his passage from Genoa
to New York, clearing Ellis
in 1920 at 18, and a photo
of his gray headstone
in a green, hilly valley.
I send it all to the clerk
and exhausted go to bed.

On my last day I sit at my carrel
despondent I've accomplished
so little this visit, just four
first-cousins twice removed
added to my chart,
my left hand cramped
from another morning
of rolling my wheelchair
over the old market's uneven
cobblestones, my head aching,
my eyes unable to focus
on the minuscule, curling,
magisterial handwriting
in Italian after 1807,
in Latin before that.

After lunch, the clerk greets me smiling.
"You made my grandfather so happy.
We finally know *our* uncle's story."

I'd almost forgotten what I'd sent.
Then, she hands me my family tree:
before, patchy in places
and stag-headed at the top,
now with two, new branches
completing the canopy
into the mid-eighteenth century
including the Zinis,
"a noble family" she tells me.
Non nobis solum nati sumus.

I'M SO TIRED OF FLOATING

in response to Charles Bonnet syndrome and
Dylan Thomas's "Do not go gentle into that good night"

I'm so tired of floating
while still sitting in a chair
and the light growing brighter
in this dark night, under a coco de mer,

waking mornings to dead relatives I've never met,
bald men, bobbed-haired women, a stern sergeant,
floating tombstones and severed heads
that congregate at the end of my bed.

Spare me my Alzheimered mother's hallucinations
after cataract surgery and macular degeneration
talking to strangers standing next to her bed
until she switched on a light, and they disappeared.

These divine or evolutionary comforts:
the approaching tunnel of light
the presence of those long dead and missed,
so I too will *go gentle into that good night.*

Just give me the right medication,
donepezil or gabapentin, also used to treat MS,
to counteract these false, epiphanic sensations
and save me from this inherited distress.

THE ESCAPE ARTIST

My partner no longer panics
when I shout "I'm on fire!"
and tear off a shirt
or kick off a shoe
at home,
on a train, or
at a reading.

I've learned to dress
in layers, wear clothes,
like cardigans, with buttons
down the front
or boots and shoes
without laces that
easily slip off.

He knows I could
leave without warning
like my church friend
from Rotterdam
who wore special boots
laced up to her knees,
with metal MS leg supports,

who after fifty years
of pain clinics,
hospital visits,
and restless nights,
silently slipped away
from her husband
as they slept side by side.

THIN STRIPS OF LATEX AND FABRIC

"Isn't it too warm to wear that?"
the wheelchair transport driver asks
staring at my surgical face mask,
his still hanging from a radio knob.

"Not as warm as being on a ventilator,"
I say. His eyes widen
in the rearview mirror
and he quickly puts his on.

I'm relieved his side window isn't open
unable to move to avoid an airflow
in the back where I'm bolted
to the floor in my wheelchair.

He reminds me of the men
who complained when I insisted
they put on a condom or leave
during the previous pandemic

who whined about a loss of feeling.
half of them dead before their thirty-fifth.
I'm grateful for those thin strips of latex or fabric
that hopefully will help me see my sixty-fifth.

À L'APOLLINAIRE?

Ayant vu la guerre…
Blessé à la tête, trépané sous le chloroforme
Ayant perdu ses meilleurs amis dans l'effroyable lutte

Having seen the war…
Wounded in the head, trepanned under chloroform
Having lost his best friends in the frightful struggle

— Guillaume Apollonaire,
from "La Jolie Rousse" (The Pretty Redhead)

Having survived the AIDS epidemic,
picked up or bagged men and their belongings,
who placed themselves in the line of fire,
held their hands, cleaned, paid the bills,
so they'd still have a place
if or when they returned,
long before the press outed
the basketball superstar
who got it from a prostitute
and suddenly Personnel decided
I needn't use unpaid leave
or personal holidays to attend funerals,

only to be killed by the COVID-19 pandemic
brought back by rich skiers, discount travelers,
and jet-setting businesspeople,
wouldn't be a joke, but an insult
having survived broken condoms, IV users, betrayal,
a man ringing my doorbell at 1 A.M.
for my partner in hospital or later dead
wanting him to join men in the park,
would be ridiculous rather than tragic

would be like Apollinaire, who having survived the guns,
the gas, the rats, the dysentery of World War I's trenches,
even a field hospital trepanation,
and sent love letters and short, matchless poems

shaped like fans, flowers, streaks of rain,
a megaphone, even a dove above a fountain,
back from the front to his lover,
finally returning home to Paris
with shrapnel in his head,
only to die shortly thereafter
from Spanish flu in his own bed.

THE WAY YOU LEFT

Ronald Linder (1930-2004)

I'm sorry the cleaner
broke the paper band
across your laundered shirt
before I could stop her.
She couldn't have known
it was one of the last things
that you touched
that touched you
that week before
you went into hospital
and never came out.

You said I was a poet
masquerading as a teacher
and you, a poet
pretending to be a doctor
eating brown-bag lunches
in the hospital parking lot while
reading Celine, Rilke, or Baudelaire,
working *The New York Times* crossword puzzle
and evenings building fractal screen savers
to feed your quick, curious mind.

You caught me cursing one evening
hurrying down the street
an hour late from work, just fifteen minutes
before the weekly writers' workshop
was due to meet in my living room.
You sat in your car's passenger seat
reading a book, the door open
your feet resting on the curb.
"You sure you want to do this?"
you asked me as you helped
put cups and saucers on the table
for tea and cookies at the break.

"This is the *only* good part of my week!"
I snapped and we both laughed. You talked
about reviving my gay literary magazine
from its five-year hibernation
and I thought only of emigration,
my company having down-sized from
seventeen to twelve to five to three offices in five years
a dozen friends and one partner dead
from AIDS complications
no teaching, insurance, or computer jobs for me
in all of San Francisco and Silicon Valley.

"There's no one left to talk to here!"
you complained when I called
from Europe every weekend
cheaper to call you for an hour
in San Francisco than friends in Amsterdam,
your family and friends dead or gone,
rising rent and bills
devouring your pension and savings
the exhausting climb up three flights
in a building with no elevator
until the third time your cancer returned,
for which, as a doctor, as a Buddhist,
you were well-prepared, having watched
countless patients die over four decades.

You divested yourself of your treasures
the reel-to-reel radio recordings:
Copland at Carnegie Hall and Garland at the Palace,
your Fritz Wünderlich opera records,
your business shirts, jackets, and raincoats
that smelled of your apartment's dust, coffee,
and the hundreds of moldering books
you'd collected over fifty years.
You'd slip two books into my suitcase
every time I came to visit
the night before I left.

In hospital you tried to distract me
from your jaundiced, skeletal torso
by pointing at the IV pump
next to your bed, its plastic cog
pushing a milky liquid through
a plastic tube without touching it.
"The most sanitary delivery method,"
you said in doctorspeak
being clinical perhaps
to give yourself distance
and make me less afraid.
Your bed pointed towards
the snowy TV screen
tuned to the History Channel
during Civil War week,
away from Richmond Beach's
miles of white breakers
outside your window.

I didn't know then
you were starving yourself
taking only liquid nutrients
to cut short your hospice stay.
On the phone a week later
I wished you "Good luck"
afraid to say "I Love You"
over the Veterans Hospital line
(in the days of "Don't Ask, Don't Tell.")
You said: "Good luck to you and Winny."
You died four days later,
no funeral or memorial service
no newspaper obituary
your ashes scattered in the Bay
under the Golden Gate.

After a decade of sixty-hour work weeks
I finally have time to listen to your tapes of

Basil Bunting, Galway Kinnell, Ai, Ned Rorem,
Ezra Pound, and Wallace Stevens.
I read through your poetry books
and write daily on my laptop
at my "soft desk," my bed,
on one of my bad days.
I wear one of your shirts
your tape carousel spins atop my stereo,
no longer frightened or angry
by my weak legs or forgetful hands
but remembering and honoring
the calm, courageous way
you lived and left.

ONE ROOM

My life has been reduced to one little room
after forty years and twenty addresses
including a San Francisco apartment
just a block from the seawall
and the constant heave and hush
of Ocean Beach's white-tipped breakers.

Just as my paternal grandmother,
her last years, had to move
downstairs in her big house
with the white, wrap-around porch,
to a room next to the kitchen garden,
where she no longer worked or walked.

Breakfast and lunch are brought on a tray
as if we're royalty or on permanent honeymoon.
We float on a cloud of classical music, painkillers,
and a soft, sunny, lemon-tangerine comforter
that carries us through the afternoon
until it's time to dress for dinner

helped out of bed by strong, foreign men
our butlers, chauffeurs, cooks, and dishwashers,
our new "husbands," our former partners long dead,
never knowing what's on the menu
but still hungry, at this point,
for food and someone's touch.

WHITE ROOM

the American Book Center, Amsterdam

A long room with white doors, shelves, walls, and floors,
flower-shaped shades on white chandeliers, and a pair
of feathered angel wings at rest on a windowsill.
People come here to browse or watch as books
are printed and bound upon request, shelves
stocked with titles on history, mythology,

psychology, and religion that promise to lift
the veil on our origins and final destinations.
I sit in my wheelchair: read, doze, muse, and write
at a table stocked with water, chocolates, and nuts,
and stacks of flyers for readings and writers' workshops.
Bright sunlight pours in through tall, many-paned windows.

ACKNOWLEDGMENTS

Thank you to the Amsterdam Quarterly Writers' Group, where these poems were discussed in earlier drafts, and to my Three Graces: Nonnie Augustine, Dianne Kellogg, and Meryl Stratford, who have aided me in my poetic labors for almost a decade. Thank you also to Jean Huets, Circling Rivers' editor, for her keen eye and judgment.

Grateful acknowledgment is also made to the publications where these poems first appeared or are scheduled to appear:

"À l'Apollinaire?" | *The Hippocrates Prize 2021*. The Hippocrates Press, 2021.

"Bethesda" | *Irreantum* 17.2 (Spring 2021).

"Don't Ask" | *The Hippocrates Prize 2022*. The Hippocrates Press, 2022

"A Drive with Mondrian," "On the Level," and "Schwarzwälder Kirschtorte" | *Immigration & Justice for Our Neighbors* (anthology). Celery City Books, 2017.

"The Familiar Stranger" | *Amsterdam Quarterly* 9 (2014).

"First Signs," "Today I Forgot" and "Why I Have Fired My Therapists" | *South Florida Poetry Journal* 1 (May 2016).

"Glasgow Meeting" | *Friends Journal* (February 2012) & *Gathered: Contemporary Quaker Poets* (anthology). Sundress Press, 2013.

"Gravity" | *Italian Americana* XL, no. 1.

"Here's Something for the Pain," "The Braces," and "The Hotel Reading" | *Kaleidoscope Magazine* 81.

"Homecoming" | *Amsterdam Quarterly* 23 (2018).

"Moonfaced Man" | *South Florida Poetry Journal* 14 (August 2019)

"No One Ever Asks" | *Friends Journal* (March 2016).

"Nobody" | *Amsterdam Quarterly* 31 (2021).

"The Rattle" | *Amsterdam Quarterly* 18 (2017).

"Suspended" | *Without a Doubt: Poems Illuminating Faith* (anthology). New York: New York Quarterly Books, 2022.

"Thin Strips of Latex and Fabric" | *Arlington Literary Journal* 153, (2021).

"Why I Have Fired My Therapists" | *Voices from the Fierce Intangible World* (anthology). SoFloPoJo Press, 2019.

"Why I Like the Ballet" | *Assaracus* 15 (2014).

Notes

"Bethesda" | John 5: 2–9. *Bible.*

"Patient Says 'No'" | Reflects catchphrase "Computer Says 'No'" in BBC TV series "Little Britain", 2003-2007.

"On The Level" | Maggie Hiufu Wong, "Friendliest/unfriendliest U.S. cities, according to Conde Nast Traveler." CNN. 7 August 2014.

"Nobody" | Odysseus and Polyphemus story in Homer's *Odyssey*, Book 9.

"Why I Didn't Use the Back Door" | *Shakers in Ohio*, by J. P. MacLean. Philadelphia: Porcupine Press, 1975.

"Inertia" | Character, Hans Biberkopf, from Alfred Döblin's novel *Berlin Alexanderplatz*. Berlin: S. Fischer Verlag, 1929.

"For Whom We Are Born" epigraph | *De Officiis (The Duties)*, by Marcus Tullius Cicero. 1:22.

"À l'Apollinaire" epigraph | "La jolie rousse," by Guillaume Apollinaire. *Calligrammes. Poems de la Paix e de la Guerre (1913-1916)*. Paris: Mercure de France, 1918.

"I'm So Tired of Floating" epigraph | "Do not go gentle into that good night," by Dylan Thomas. *Collected Poems 1934-1952*. New York: New Directions Press, 1971.

CPSIA information can be obtained
at www.ICGtesting.com
Printed in the USA
JSHW052311210922
30834JS00002B/181